Not Without A
FIGHT

Dr. John R. Adolph

This book is dedicated to

The Lord of Hosts who is our God of Battle

My beautiful wife, Dorrie and my wonderful children, Sumone and Jonathan

The loving memory of my father and mother who now rest upon the lap of God awaiting the certain sound of the trumpet in the rapture

My supportive siblings, Pastor Seymour V. Adolph, Jr., Nell, and Ron

My phenomenal staff at the church whose love and labor never cease to amaze me

My committed church leaders who collaborate with me in Kingdom Building endeavors

The magnificent members of the Antioch Missionary Baptist Church of Beaumont, Texas

In addition, most importantly, to the men and women of our Nations Armed Forces who give so graciously of themselves to protect the boundaries and borders of the country that we love

Dr. John R. Adolph

Table of Contents

Group Encounter Week 3

Daily Devotionals Week 3

Group Encounter Week 4

Daily Devotionals Week 4

Dr. John R. Adolph

Don't Just Fight To The End Fight To Win!

To be a real Christian means that you are engaged in battle. We have a very real adversary whose aim is our destruction. The enemy will use any tactic, strategy, or happening to cause the faithful to lose heart and to become weary enough to welcome defeat and throw in the towel. The great news for the believer however, is this, we may have a real enemy, but we have an awesome advocate. His name is Jesus Christ, Son of the living God! Our Christ is not just an ever-present deity helping us get to the end; He is the Lord of Hosts, the God of battle who is empowering us so that we fight well and fight to win!

You are about to embark upon a 40-day journey of excitement! For the next six weeks, you will be sharing God's Word with those that are in your group and or class. Of course, you could do this study alone, but this study will come out greater if you share it with family, friends, and people that you love. With this in mind, once a week gather with the people that make up your group. Design a set place and time for you to meet. Each group session should last no more than an hour and a half. You should have a DVD that contains the video presentations used for this study (if you are not the group leader your leader should have the disc) and a workbook in hand that consists of group sessions designed to enrich you and individual devotionals composed to inspire you.

Start each group session by following the directions given at the start of each chapter. When the group sessions have been concluded, time will be allotted for dialogue and discussion concerning the lesson.

During the week, you will need to carve out of your busy schedule at least 7 minutes a day for God. This will be your devotional time. This can happen at any point in your day, but make it happen at the same time every day no matter what. During this 7-minute period, you will read the letter of James and write some of your thoughts in your journal. You will find this time of journaling each day both healing and refreshing.

With this in mind, never forget that the Bible is the greatest book that history will ever have in its possession. It is God-breathed, spiritually dictated, and divinely inspired. It is a portion of the mind of God on paper, it is bread for the hungry, a light for those in darkness, healing for the wounded, strength for the weak, direction for the lost, a constitution for those that are a part of God's Kingdom on earth and a road map to victory for every believer that will live its principles and practice its precepts. Therefore, a crucial key to victory in your destiny is to feed your soul God's Word daily.

Your life is about to change for the better! As you study God's Word over the next few weeks, you are going to encounter Jesus Christ in some wonderful ways. You will see that in sin He is a Savior, in darkness He is a light, in confusion He is direction, in bondage He is a liberator, in sickness He is a physician, in times of hurt He is a healer, in loneliness He is a steadfast companion, in weakness He is your strength, in death He is your life and in life He is your victory. Jesus Christ is our victorious, vicarious King! The finished work of the Lord Jesus Christ at Calvary sealed victory on the battleground of life with a win against sin and satan for us for the last time.

Fight to Win!

But thanks be to God, which giveth us victory through our Lord Jesus Christ (I Corinthians 15:57)

Dr. John R. Adolph

Group Encounter Week 1

FIGHT AGAINST DESPAIR
James 1:1-4

Intelligence Briefing

1. Take this moment to introduce yourself to everyone in your group.
2. Share an experience that you have had in your life that made you feel hopeless.
3. Discuss how you fought to get through this period of your life.

Five Battle Strategies: Video Presentation

A. The key to handling despair is _____.

B. No one _____ everything about God.

C. Patience means to be _____.

D. To be _____ means to be complete.

E. You need nothing when you have _____.

The Training Op

1. What are some places the world finds joy?
2. Where should a believers joy come from?
3. How is joy increased?

The Basics: Psalms 30:5. Discuss it. Memorize it.

Prepare For Battle: Closing Prayer

Dr. John R. Adolph

Daily Devotionals Week 1

-Day 1-

Fight Like Your Mind Is Made Up

OPERATIONS MANUAL

If any of you lack wisdom, let him ask of God, that giveth to all men liberally, and upbraideth not; and it shall be given him. But let him ask in faith, nothing wavering. For he that wavereth is like a wave of the sea driven with the wind and tossed. For let not that man think that he shall receive any thing of the Lord. A double-minded man is unstable in all his ways. (James 1:5-8)

STRATEGIC INTELLIGENCE

The only way to fight as a soldier in Jesus Christ is to have your mind made up. The worse person in the world to fight with is someone who is not sure that they want to be involved in the battle. Listen, being a real Christian puts you in harm's way. If that frightens you then this walk of faith in Jesus Christ may not be for you. There are times your life will see attacks from the enemy. There will be moments when sickness, disease, death, and discomfort will come your way. That is not the time to break down or retreat. That is the time to stand up and declare that my mind is made up! I will follow Jesus Christ no matter what!

The great news is that you have superior intelligence within your grasp. You have God's wisdom at your disposal. He is in the

Control Room waiting and willing to give you directions regarding what to do, how to do and when to do. It is what the Bible calls wisdom. How do you get wisdom from God? Just ask and He will flood your heart, mind, and soul.

Remember this, doubt distracts and destroys, but wisdom grants the vicar spiritual victory!

Wisdom connected to a made up mind spells victory everyday of your life.

THE INWARD BATTLE

The real war happens in your mind. Here are some questions you should answer as you spend this devotional moment with God.

- Is your mind really made up?

- What are some things that cause you to doubt God?

- What has God done in your past that proves that He is with you when no one else is?

TACTICAL WEAPONS AND WARFARE

O God of heaven empower me this day to rid my soul of needless doubt and fill me with wisdom from above. Grant me the faith to use the wisdom that you give me and the willingness to never ever doubt your ability, veracity, authority, or sovereignty ever again. I thank you for a made up mind right this very moment. For Christ I live and for Christ I will die! In the name of Jesus, Amen!

-Day 2-

Fight Like You Will Win

OPERATIONS MANUAL

Let the brother of low degree rejoice in that he is exalted: but the rich, in that he is made low: because as the flower of the grass he shall pass away. For the sun is no sooner risen with a burning heat, but it withereth the grass, and the flower thereof falleth, and the grace of the fashion of it perisheth: so also shall the rich man fade away in his ways.
(James 1:9-11)

STRATEGIC INTELLIGENCE

There is a huge difference between weakness and meekness, humility and stupidity, God's way and your way. As you do battle, there are times when you will want to do things your way. Here is some news for you to both retain and maintain, as long as you are on life's battlefield, be humble by way of decision and God will exalt you by way of promotion! In short, you win, even if it is over the rich.

James compares the rich (oppressor) to those of low decree (the oppressed). He reminds those that look like they are at the bottom that the tables will soon turn and what is at the bottom will be lifted to the top. He then uses a beautiful mental picture for you to consider. James illustrates this principle like this, the sunrises, and the flowers fade because the heat drives them away. Like the sunrises, so it is that the Son has risen. In addition, when He returns the rich (those who use their resources to oppress the poor) will fade and those who are humble will win in the end!

Here is the conclusion of the matter, fight like the one who will win because in Christ you have already won!

THE INWARD BATTLE

Take a moment and read Psalms 37:1-5.

How did this passage make your soul feel?

In James 1:9-11 who are the rich?

Have you ever fought a battle your way and ended in defeat?

Take a moment and reflect on what happened.

Have you ever had a fight that you released to the Lord and He stood for you and gave you victory? How did this make your heart feel?

Keep this in mind: if you stand for God in faith, He will stand for you in battle!

TACTICAL WEAPONS AND WARFARE

Lord forgive me for trying to fight my own battles. I am guilty of doing it and I humbly admit it. Be my Lord of Hosts and fight for me! I will humble myself so that you can exalt me. I will stand for you, so that you can fight for me. Thank you for the victory you have given me in Jesus Christ, Amen!

-Day 3-

Fight Temptation And Hold Out!

OPERATIONS MANUAL

Blessed is the man that endureth temptation: for when he is tried, he shall receive the crown of life, which the Lord hath promised to them that love him. Let no man say when he is tempted, I am tempted of God: for God cannot be tempted with evil, neither tempteth he any man: but every man is tempted, when he is drawn away of his own lust, and enticed. Then when lust hath conceived, it bringeth forth sin: and sin, when it is finished, bringeth forth death. (James 1:12-15)

STRATEGIC INTELLIGENCE

Temptation is one thing and testing is another. Temptation (pirosmos-to be lured by the devil) is a demonic operation designed for your ruin. Testing is a divine examination designed for your growth and betterment. In short, temptation is from the devil and it is meant for your destruction. Testing is from the Lord and it is designed for your development. At times, they both feel and look the same.

So how can you tell the difference between the two of them while you are on the battlefield? During times of testing God is silent! Like a great Commander and Chief, He speaks during times of preparation, but during the test, He has nothing to say.

During times of temptation, God gives you warnings! In a still small voice, He speaks to you.

James reminds us that all of us will be tempted. In fact, he says that we will be "drawn away by our own lust and enticed." This phrase is aquatic in its make-up. It is used when a fish is lured to eat bait that is attached to a hook. The fish loves the bait, but what he cannot see is the deadly trap of the hook that will lead to his demise. Testing then produces the treasure that is within you. Temptation is a trap sent from hell to destroy you. Hold out during times of temptation, its end is lethal and can be fatal if you are not careful.

THE INWARD BATTLE

What is the difference between temptation and testing?

James declares that every human being is tempted. What are some things that cause you to be tempted? Be honest.

The key to tackling temptation is simple. Choose being blessed over being cursed. Re-read verse 12. The first word is "blessed." If you desire to be blessed you chose it.

Your decision to follow Jesus will make other decisions for you. Make your decision to live only to please the Master and old temptations will not tempt you as they used to.

TACTICAL WEAPONS AND WARFARE

God in heaven, help me to hold out in the face of temptation, especially when I am weak. Hold me up in the faith and keep me strong is my earnest prayer. Thank you Jesus for speaking to me when I am being tempted. Hold me while I am being tested. In the name of my risen Master, Jesus, I pray, Amen!

Dr. John R. Adolph

-Day 4-

Fight With A Chip On Your Shoulder!

OPERATIONS MANUAL

Do not err, my beloved brethren. Every good gift and every perfect gift is from above, and cometh down from the Father of lights, with whom is no variableness, neither shadow of turning. Of his own will begat he us with the word of truth, that we should be a kind of first fruits of his creatures. (James 1:16-18)

STRATEGIC INTELLIGENCE

When you rise in the morning to the blessing of a new day, when your eyes open, when your feet hit the ground, you should get up knowing that the same God that made the sunrise, the moon glow and the stars twinkle caused you to rise as well! The power here is that if God made the sun rise after having it set, there is nothing that you can face in the course of the day that He cannot handle for you. This should put a little chip on your shoulder.

Not long ago, I was on a turbulent flight from Chicago back to Houston. I was sitting next to a kid who was playing and having a good ole time while the aircraft bobbled in the air at 37,000 feet above the earth, like a kite in the wind. The passengers and flight crew were in shock. The kid was at play. After we landed, the pilot made his way to my row. He looked at the kid and said "Tiger are you alright?" To which the boy replied, "Yeah dad I fly with a chip on my shoulder!"

If this kid could fly with a chip on his shoulder because his dad was the pilot, you should be able to fight with a chip on your shoulder because your Father is the one that holds every plane in the air!

Get this and hold onto it, to fight with a chip on your shoulder means to approach each day knowing that God is on your side and He can handle anything that comes your way.

THE INWARD BATTLE

What are some things that you often worry about?

At what point are you going to put those things in the hand of God and let Him handle them for you?

Read Proverbs 3:5-7

If the enemy of trust is doubt, then the advocate of trust must be belief. What are some things that you really believe about God? Be specific.

If God only gave you what you could believe Him for, what would you have?

TACTICAL WEAPONS AND WARFARE

Lord Jesus there are times that I worry too much and trust too little. Forgive me. Today is the start of a new walk of trust for me. I am deciding to trust you with all that I am and all that I have. I trust you with both my history and my destiny. I belong to you and you belong to me. In Jesus' name, Amen!

-Day 5-

Fight By Obeying Orders!

OPERATIONS MANUAL

Wherefore, my beloved brethren, let every man be swift to hear, slow to speak, slow to wrath: for the wrath of man worketh not the righteousness of God. Wherefore lay apart all filthiness and superfluity of naughtiness, and receive with meekness the engrafted word, which is able to save your souls. (James 1:19-21)

STRATEGIC INTELLIGENCE

Soldiers follow orders or people die. It is just that simple. To fail at following orders at the least can gain you a military reprimand and at the worse a dishonorable discharge, which is a permanent scar on the life of any soldier that has sought to serve their country. If the orders say go to Germany, that soldier is going to Germany. If the orders say go to Iraq that soldier is on a plane within a few days if not hours headed due east. Moreover, if the orders say get to Alaska, no matter how cold it is there, they will live in Alaska. Why? Soldiers obey orders!

As believers in the Lord's army, we too obey orders. James gives a list of commands and they must be followed without fail or else. He says be quick to hear. This means to be quiet and receive the instructions. Secondly, he says be slow to speak. This does not mean to talk slowly, but it means to speak only when you need to. This is because in the Hebrew culture too much talking would lend itself to lying at some point. And be slow to get mad. In short, listen up, shut up, speak up, and handle up on your attitude.

Get rid of things that are holding you down and get ready for the Word to be planted in your soul so that you might be able to survive each battle and stand in victory.

THE INWARD BATTLE

What are some orders that you really need to follow and do?

Spiritual warfare is serious business. Read Ephesians 6:10-20. What does this reading say to your mind?

If God called you to do a special assignment for Him, what would you do? Is He calling you right now? If so, why have not you responded and said yes?

TACTICAL WEAPONS AND WARFARE

Eternal and everlasting God it is my desire to obey your every command. However, there are times that I fall short. For this sin, I seek your mercy, which suits me and your grace that saves me from your wrath. God give me the strength to do exactly what you have called me to do and prepare me to receive your Word so that I can fight the good fight of faith and stand victorious when time is over for me. In the name of Jesus I petition you, Amen!

Group Encounter Week 2

THIS IS WHERE THE REAL FIGHT HAPPENS
James 1:22-25

Intelligence Briefing

1. Take prayer requests from everyone in your group. Whisper prayers for everyone.
2. Have you ever struggled with doing the Word? What was your greatest struggle?

Five Battle Strategies: Video Presentation

A. To do the _____ requires action.

B. To _____ and not do is to be disobedient.

C. Learn to work on the _____ in the mirror.

D. A doer is always _____.

E. Hearing and Doing requires_____.

The Training Op

1. Look at yourself in the mirror. What do you see?
2. Make a list of things the Word says you should do. Are you doing it yet?

The Basics: Read Phil. 4:13 Memorize it.

Prepare For Battle: Closing Prayer

Daily Devotionals Week 2

-Day 1-

Fight For The Benefit Of Others!

<u>*OPERATIONS MANUAL*</u>

If any man among you seem to be religious, and bridleth not his tongue, but deceiveth his own heart, this man's religion is vain. Pure religion and undefiled before God and the Father is this, To visit the fatherless and widows in their affliction, and to keep himself unspotted from the world.
(James 1:26-27)

<u>*STRATEGIC INTELLIGENCE*</u>

Tom Hanks is fabulous in the award-winning movie Forrest Gump. He is born to a single parent mother in Greenbo, Alabama and is considered to be academically challenged. In short, he is supposed to be a little slow. He somehow makes it through high school, runs a football through college and enters the United States Army. The shocker of the movie is when Forest wins the Congressional Medal of Honor. You see, while on the battlefield, Forest was known for saving his friends. Though wounded himself, he is soldier enough to go back into hostile territory for the good of others.

When we consider these verses in James, it is as if he has seen the movie too. For the greatest of soldiers are not those who fight for themselves. The greatest men and women on the field of battle are those fighting for the soldier next to them and for the people back home.

Here is the real deal, there are times a father has to fight for his son, a mother has to fight for her daughter, a believer has to fight to win a sinner to Christ, an earnest politician has to fight to get a bill passed, a Pastor has to fight for the good of the Gospel and a believer has to fight in prayer for the healing of some child who has just been diagnosed with a disease. Fighting for others is what we do!

James says it so clearly in this devotional segment. Fight to control what comes from you (your tongue) and fight for the less fortunate around you (children and the elderly). James says when you fight for them you have religion that is worthwhile.

THE INWARD BATTLE

Here is a question for you to ponder today. Whom are you fighting for? Why are you fighting for them?

The Christian faith is about knowing and doing. What have you been doing lately to help someone other than yourself?

Prepare to do a simple service project. Look within your family first. Find a child or an elder and do a kind gesture for them. No matter how they receive it, just do it. Then tell the Lord, it was done just to make Him happy.

TACTICAL WEAPONS AND WARFARE

Jesus I desire to please you. I want to make you happy with me. It is my desire to have a relationship with you that makes my religion worthwhile. Use my hands to serve you, use my heart to please you and give me the strength to fight for those who cannot fight for themselves. Show me what to do and I will do it for your glory. In Jesus' name, Amen!

Dr. John R. Adolph

-Day 2-

Fight Against Favoritism!

OPERATIONS MANUAL

My brethren, have not the faith of our Lord Jesus Christ, the Lord of glory, with respect of persons. For if there come unto your assembly a man with a gold ring, in goodly apparel, and there come in also a poor man in vile raiment; and ye have respect to him that weareth the gay clothing, and say unto him, Sit thou here in a good place; and say to the poor, Stand thou there, or sit here under my footstool: are ye not then partial in yourselves, and are become judges of evil thoughts? Hearken, my beloved brethren, Hath not God chosen the poor of this world rich in faith, and heirs of the kingdom which he hath promised to them that love him? But ye have despised the poor. Do not rich men oppress you, and draw you before the judgment seats? Do not they blaspheme that worthy name by the which ye are called? If ye fulfill the royal law according to the scripture, Thou shalt love thy neighbor as thyself, ye do well: but if ye have respect to persons, ye commit sin, and are convinced of the law as transgressors. (James 2:1-9)

STRATEGIC INTELLIGENCE

One Sunday the Pastor of a mega-church decided to do something different for his sermon. Instead of coming to church, as he normally would have, he pretended to be a homeless vagabond. He wore tattered and torn clothing. He did not shave, leaving his face filled with razor stubble. He did not drive his nice sedan he walked up to the church. And, to his surprise, he was treated horribly. No one greeted him, no one shook his hand, and no one offered him a seat in the cathedral. To make matters worse, no one wanted to sit near him.

When it was time for the sermon, he stepped out of the congregation and approached the microphone and security guards and deacons sought to stop him. Finally, one of the deacons recognized him and said to the others "It's Pastor!" The Pastor took the microphone and read St. Matthew 25:31-46. A hush fell over the crowd. It was then that he told them in God's house and amongst God's people, there are no VIP's!

Keep this in mind; God is no respecter of persons!

THE INWARD BATTLE

Be honest, have you ever judged someone based on his or her outer appearance?

How do you feel when someone who is less fortunate than you, enters your presence?

Have you ever been the person that was the one with less around those with more? How did they make you feel?

TACTICAL WEAPONS AND WARFARE

Lord please help me to treat all people like they matter. Help me to become a conduit of love so that when people meet me they encounter you. In Jesus' name, Amen and Amen!

-Day 3-

Fight Like Mercy Is Your Best Friend!

OPERATIONS MANUAL

For whosoever shall keep the whole law, and yet offend in one point, he is guilty of all. For he that said, Do not commit adultery, said also, Do not kill. Now if thou commit no adultery, yet if thou kill, thou art become a transgressor of the law. So speak ye, and so do, as they that shall be judged by the law of liberty. For he shall have judgment without mercy, that hath shewed no mercy; and mercy rejoiceth against judgment. (James 2:10-13)

STRATEGIC INTELLIGENCE

If you want mercy from God, you have to give mercy to those who need it from you. If you do not give it, you will never get it. It is just that simple.

Often times we celebrate the wrong doings of others that have made the news and the media highlights. Can you imagine what your life would look like if everybody knew the complete truth about who you really are? How would you feel if your dirty laundry was aired on CNN next week? It would be crushing, embarrassing, heartbreaking, and life altering.

Get this; God does not need a satellite in outer space to record what you have done. He does not need a reporter to inform Him of your failures and sins. He knows! He watched! He was there! Do you feel a little uneasy yet? You should. "All have sinned" (Romans 3:23a) is what the Bible declares. However, instead of giving you justice, God has granted you mercy!

Therefore, mercy is not a ticket to sin freely; it is a force that should make you want to live holy. This is why you should fight as if mercy is your best friend, because mercy is a friend indeed!

THE INWARD BATTLE

Here is a meditation question that should bring tears to your eyes if you really ponder it seriously. What sins have you committed that if discovered would destroy you? Now hold on to this reality, God has granted you mercy! How does it feel?

Mercy received should produce the strength you need to never to do some things ever again. What sins do you vow never to commit anymore?

If mercy had a price tag how much do you think it would costs? Get this, it cost Jesus His life, this is why He requires your life in exchange.

TACTICAL WEAPONS AND WARFARE

Lord today I give you all that I am so that I can receive all that you are. I am a sinner and I really need your mercy. Help me O God to grant mercy to those who have wronged me so that I may receive mercy from you without limit. And, cause me to fight as if mercy is the best friend I will ever have, in Jesus' mighty name, Amen!

-Day 4-

Fight As If Your Faith Is On Fire!

OPERATIONS MANUAL

What doth it profit, my brethren, though a man say he hath faith, and have not works? Can faith save him? If a brother or sister be naked, and destitute of daily food, and one of you say unto them, depart in peace, be ye warmed and filled; notwithstanding ye give them not those things which are needful to the body; what doth it profit? Even so faith, if it hath not works, is dead, being alone Yea, a man may say, thou hast faith, and I have works: shew me thy faith without thy works, and I will shew thee my faith by my works. Thou believest that there is one God; thou doest well: the devils also believe, and tremble. But wilt thou know, O vain man, that faith without works is dead? (James 2:14-20)

STRATEGIC INTELLIGENCE

Faith is an action word. It means to do something! It is not just the resolve of what you believe; it is also the concrete function that produces how you behave. Not long ago, while visiting a city on the west coast, I took notice of a woman feeding homeless people out of the trunk of her car. The line of transients was wrapped around the automobile. Many looked to be drug addicted, some appeared to be dangerous, and a few of them I am certain were running from the law. However, that did not stop this woman at all. She was feeding these people until her food ran out. As we got near her trunk, she had a huge sign dangling from her bumper that read, "I'm through talking, and I am all action! Faith without works is dead!"

The writings of James clearly inspired this woman and it should do the same thing for you. At some point, you should desire to do what the Bible says to do. Talk is cheap, chatter is not necessary, but when your faith has arms, legs and a heart everything around you will start to move heavenward for the glory of our God.

Keep this in mind, if you show me your faith, I will show you your works. Your works will always look like your faith does!

THE INWARD BATTLE

Some people in life have a bucket list. This is a list of things that they would like to do before they die. Believers should have a Faith List. A list of things that they would like to do for God before they die. If you had a Faith List, what would be on it? What are some things you would like to do for God before you die?

Have you ever wondered what the hand of the Lord looks like? Take a moment and look down your arm. His hand is starring you in the face. Here is the question: what are you going to do with it?

Do a simple project. Help someone this week that you know cannot help you back. When you have finished doing it, whisper to God and tell Him, that you did it just to make Him smile.

TACTICAL WEAPONS AND WARFARE

God of grace and Lord of mercy, I approach you this moment asking you to please stand with me as I put my faith into action. I seek to serve you in a more meaningful way. God from the top of my head to the bottom of my feet, use me until you are satisfied. My hands are yours, my mind is yours, my heart is yours, and all that I have is yours! Use me please so that my faith and my works make you happy with me. In your name, Jesus, I pray! Amen!

Dr. John R. Adolph

Day 5-

Fight Like Those Who Have Crazy Faith!

OPERATIONS MANUAL

Was not Abraham our father justified by works, when he had offered Isaac his son upon the altar? Seest thou how faith wrought with his works, and by works was faith made perfect? And the scripture was fulfilled which saith, Abraham believed God, and it was imputed unto him for righteousness: and he was called the Friend of God. Ye see then how that by works a man is justified, and not by faith only. Likewise also was not Rahab the harlot justified by works, when she had received the messengers, and had sent them out another way? For as the body without the spirit is dead, so faith without works is dead also. (James 2:21-26)

STRATEGIC INTELLIGENCE

Faith in God is one thing, but crazy faith in the Lord Jesus Christ is something very different. Crazy faith is the thing that made Moses walk into the pristine palace of Pharaoh with a stick in his hand to declare that all of the Hebrews needed to be released from bondage; it is the thing that would make Peter get out of a boat while it was in the water and try to walk on the waves to go to Jesus; and, it is the thing that made James lift two great faith stories for us to consider in his letter, Abraham and Rahab respectively.

Crazy faith is faith that trusts God blindly. Abraham had it when he took his only son Isaac to a mountain and offered him up as a sacrifice to God. Crazy faith not only trusts God blindly, but it believes in God's ability. Rahab had it when she told the two spies that you represent the God of heaven and I will help you if you spare my family and me.

The battle for the believer in Jesus Christ cannot be won with faith that is common and conservative. It must be a faith that is confident and completely crazy. A faith that says things like, "For to me to live is Christ and to die is gain" (Phil. 1:21), "If I perish, let me perish" (Esther 4:16) and "All of my appointed time will I wait until my change comes' (Job 14:14). Crazy faith is how we fight and it is the faith that we gain victory over the enemy with!

Remember this, when you show God crazy faith, He grants you unusual favor and amazing grace!

THE INWARD BATTLE

The enemy of crazy faith is common sense. Has God ever led you to do something, it took crazy faith to do it, and your common sense talked you out it? What was it?

Doubt can often times cripple faith and weaken it. What are some areas of your faith that doubt weakens?

The only way to strengthen faith is by hearing. Read Romans 10:17. What does this say to your heart?

TACTICAL WEAPONS AND WARFARE

Lord give me the kind of faith that Abraham and Rahab had. Increase it every day by allowing me to hear your Word and do it. Thank you for my increase in faith and my overflow in blessing. In the name of Jesus, I petition you. Amen!

Dr. John R. Adolph

Group Encounter Week 3

FIGHT WITH THE WORDS THAT COME FROM YOUR MOUTH

James 3:1-2

Intelligence Briefing

1. Have a moment of welcome and prayer. Discuss a time when you were crushed by something someone said about you.
2. How important are words to you?

Five Battle Strategies: Video Presentation

A. Not many should be _____.
B. Teachers use_____ and words have power.
C. Words can be offensive when used _____.
D. Control your _____ and control your life.
E. What you _____ is what you will soon see.

The Training Op

1. Why are words so important to us?
2. List words that damage people every day.
3. How do words encourage you? Discuss it.

The Basics: Prov. 18:21-Discuss it. Memorize it.

Prepare For Battle: Closing Prayer

Daily Devotionals Week 3

-Day 1-

Fight For Control Of Your Mouth!

<u>*OPERATIONS MANUAL*</u>

Behold, we put bits in the horses' mouths, that they may obey us; and we turn about their whole body. Behold also the ships, which though they be so great, and are driven of fierce winds, yet are they turned about with a very small helm, whithersoever the governor listeth. (James 3:3-4)

<u>*STRATEGIC INTELLIGENCE*</u>

One of the things you have to admire about those persons who are in the armed forces of our country is their discipline. The training that they receive requires it. In boot camp the Drill Sergeant speaks, everyone else listens, and responds with an emphatic, "yes drill sergeant!" In short, lesson number one in the military is to control that mouth of yours. You speak when you are spoken to and that is that!

As believers in the army of our God, we must control our tongues. If you lack control of your mouth, you will never learn, never grow, struggle to develop, and prove to be unteachable. James is about to give the longest discourse in the Bible regarding the human tongue. For 12 verses in this small letter James is about to discuss the power of the tongue.

Lesson number one is learning how to control it because ultimately it controls you. He compares the tongue to a bit in a horse's mouth and the tiny rudder on a huge ship at sea. What do the two of them have in common? They both determine the direction that the object travels. Like the bit in the mouth of a horse and the rudder on a ship, your tongue determines your direction and ultimate outcome.

Today's lesson is powerful. Control that mouth of yours!

THE INWARD BATTLE

What do a horse's bit and a ship's rudder have in common?

How powerful do you think human speech really is?

Read Proverbs 18:21. What does this verse say to your mind?

A moment of total honesty: do you have a problem with your mouth from time to time? If so, what are you going to do about it?

TACTICAL WEAPONS AND WARFARE

God help me to control my tongue. I realize that there are times I use it and it hurts people. There even times I use it and I cause damage to myself. From now on, I pray that you would give me the strength to use my tongue to bless, empower, exhort, encourage, and inspire others and myself. In the name of Jesus, Amen!

-Day 2-

Fight By Knowing When To Shut Up!

OPERATIONS MANUAL

Even so the tongue is a little member, and boasteth great things. Behold, how great a matter a little fire kindleth! And the tongue is a fire, a world of iniquity: so is the tongue among our members, that it defileth the whole body, and setteth on fire the course of nature; and it is set on fire of hell. For every kind of beasts, and of birds, and of serpents, and of things in the sea, is tamed, and hath been tamed of mankind: but the tongue can no man tame; it is an unruly evil, full of deadly poison. (James 3:5-8)

STRATEGIC INTELLIGENCE

Nearly a decade ago, an older married couple came to me for counseling that had been married for nearly two decades. The man walked in happy and the woman walked in drooped. After a whisper of prayer, I asked them how I could help them. The man replied we are having some real problems. My wife is unhappy. As she is sitting in her seat, she is drooping but lifts her hand like a student in the class that needs to be recognized for offering a reply. Therefore, I kindly ask her to speak. She said, "Rev. we don't need to be in here wasting your time with all of this. We would be fine if he just stops killing me with the words that come from his mouth. He shoots me with his comments and expects me to be happy living with him. Living with him is like sleeping with a sniper that has a loaded gun with a sensitive trigger. I am wounded because I have been hit and it hurts!"

I asked her to be excused and I gave this wonderful older man that I love and admire some godly advice. Here it is, know when to shut up. Your tongue is killing your wife.

James describes the human tongue as a fire! It is amazing, fire that is in control and used well can cook a meal that will bless you. However, fire that is out of control can burn the whole house down. It is all in how the fire is used.

Remember this, spiritual maturity is not displayed when you tell someone a piece of your mind, but when you close your mouth and allow God's peace to rule your mind!

THE INWARD BATTLE

Why do you think James says your tongue can be just like fire?

Have you ever set something ablaze with words that came from your mouth?

Have you ever been crushed by words from other people? How did it make you feel?

TACTICAL WEAPONS AND WARFARE

Lord forgive me for the words that I have used before that have hurt people. Teach me O God to use my mouth in a godly way. Strengthen me in this area because I need it. In Jesus' name, I make this plea. Amen!

-Day 3-

Fight For Blessing, Run From Cursing!

OPERATIONS MANUAL

Therewith bless we God, even the Father; and therewith curse we men, which are made after the similitude of God. Out of the same mouth proceedeth blessing and cursing. My brethren, these things ought not so to be. Doth a fountain send forth at the same place sweet water and bitter? Can the fig tree, my brethren, bear olive berries? either a vine, figs? so can no fountain both yield salt water and fresh.
(James 3:9-12)

STRATEGIC INTELLIGENCE

This section is only for Christians who still use profanity. If you can honestly say that I do not use such language ever, simply read this section to stay safe. However, if you are reading this section and you can still toss some expletives together when you need to; if you only let one slip every once in a while or if foul language flows from your lips like water from a faucet this chapter is loaded just for you.

James says stop! Cut it off! Delete those words from your mental Rolodex! Get rid of those known tongues! It is displeasing to God! Why? It dishonors the Lord for a converted heart to produced unconverted language. You see, what is in the well of the heart comes out of the bucket of the mouth. Imagine walking up to a beautiful water faucet thirsty. You stop to get a drink and what comes out is water from a drainage ditch. Imagine what it would feel like if you downloaded a good app and opened it and a virus attacked your equipment. You would be furious! That is how God feels when a converted heart produces profane language. It just should not be.

Here is the Biblical lesson for you to consider today, if you still use profanity stop.

THE INWARD BATTLE

If you are saved and still use profanity, there are normally some things that trigger it. What are some things that push you to the edge? Be honest.

Do you really love the Lord with your whole heart? If so, then why does your mouth still speak profanity? Your heart is a well and your mouth is a bucket. Your mouth and your heart are connected. When you love God with your whole heart, you will have a language free of expletives.

Read St. Matthew 22:37, St. Luke 10:27 and Deuteronomy 6:5. What do all of these verses have in common?

TACTICAL WEAPONS AND WARFARE

Lord, I love you with my whole heart. I humbly ask you to let the words of my mouth be a reflection of the warmth I have in my heart for you each time I speak. God if my heart is broken, heal it so that my speech may help to heal others. In the name of Jesus Christ, I petition you. Amen!

-Day 4-

Fight With Meekness!

OPERATIONS MANUAL

Who is a wise man and endued with knowledge among you? let him shew out of a good conversation his works with meekness of wisdom. (James 3:13)

STRATEGIC INTELLIGENCE

In every branch of the armed forces, they have secret weapons. These weapons are not publically advertised. You do not see them used during recruiting commercials. They are used in the heat of battle to bring forth victory. One of the greatest secret weapons of a saint is meekness. Meekness is simply power under control. For the believer in Jesus Christ who is a soldier for God, meekness is best defined as your entire life under the complete control of Almighty God. He gives the commands and you give the obedience. He tells you what must be done and you in obedience do it. He orders it and you fulfill it. This is meekness and it is powerful. Never forget this principle, what makes meekness powerful is that it invokes the law of redemptive reversal each time it is used!

Jesus used it masterfully at Calvary. Many thought Jesus was weak on the cross. People from the crowd yelled at Him that fateful day to get Himself down. However, Jesus remained on the cross not out of weakness but out of meekness. He knew that if through meekness He endured the crucifixion, the law of redemptive reversal would apply and He would encounter a resurrection. This is why He had to get up on Sunday morning! Meekness always wins!

If you want God to put you at the top be meek and go to the bottom and He will exalt you in due time. If you want to be first, voluntarily go to the end and you will discover that the last shall be first!

James says if you are wise, learn to be meek and you will never lose.

THE INWARD BATTLE

The enemy of meekness is human pride. Have you ever seen your pride push you in the wrong direction? What happened?

Meekness and humility run the same direction. In what ways has being humble blessed you?

Read 1 Peter 5:6. What does this say to your soul?

TACTICAL WEAPONS AND WARFARE

God there are times that my pride can get the best of me. Please I pray forgive me. I bow my head and bend my knee to you because I know that without you I am nothing. O God, I praise you for the law of redemptive reversal. You have used meekness to exalt me and humility to bless me. I earnestly ask that you let wisdom, meekness and humility be my garments of victory and my medals of honor. In the name of Jesus, Amen!

-Day 5-

Fight For The Sake Of Peace!

OPERATIONS MANUAL

But if ye have bitter envying and strife in your hearts, glory not, and lie not against the truth. This wisdom descendeth not from above, but is earthly, sensual, devilish. For where envying and strife is, there is confusion and every evil work. But the wisdom that is from above is first pure, then peaceable, gentle, and easy to be intreated, full of mercy and good fruits, without partiality and without hypocrisy. And the fruit of righteousness is sown in peace of them that make peace. (James 3:14-18)

STRATEGIC INTELLIGENCE

Whenever and wherever you find envy, strife, chaos, and confusion it is the work of our adversary the devil. It is just that simple. His modus operandi is division and he seeks to divide and conquer the body of Christ on earth. Nevertheless, when you find peace, good fruit, righteousness, and truth it is the work of our God, our triumphant King, Jesus Christ!

While you are here on earth, you must recognize that this is enemy territory. Moreover, there are some things that we must fight in the spirit to produce for the cause of Christ. Peace is one of those things. This is why Jesus taught in the Beatitudes that the peacemakers would be blessed! It is because making peace takes an effort to destroy evil plots and plans of the enemy.

When you are the peacemaker in your marriage, healing comes your way. When you fight for peace in your heart regarding those who have hurt you deeply, you will have forgiveness embedded in your soul. In addition, when you fight for peace in the midst of total chaos for those who are being unjustly mistreated by systems that are corrupt, you reap blessing on yourself.

God gives peace and it is made by those who are peacemakers who seek to destroy the division of the enemy and bring unity to the body of Christ.

THE INWARD BATTLE

James makes a list of things that can work against peace. One of those things is bitter envying in your own heart. Examine your heart and ask God if there is any envy that you need removed today.

Have you ever seen chaos destroy a family? What about a friendship? What about marriage? What happened?

What do you think the role of peacemaker is? How can God use you to be one who makes peace in times when chaos and confusion seem to be winning the battle?

TACTICAL WEAPONS AND WARFARE

Lord Jesus make me a peacemaker whenever and wherever the enemy seeks to produce chaos near me. Most importantly, God if I harbor any envy, anger, jealousy, or contempt for anyone I pray that you would remove it. I have no desire for it any longer. I love you Lord. In Jesus' name, I pray, Amen!

Group Encounter Week 4

FIGHT THROUGH YOUR PERSONAL HANG-UP'S
James 4:1-3

Intelligence Briefing

1. Read Rom. 3:23. Discuss it openly.
2. What are some of your hang-ups?

Five Battle Strategies: Video Presentation

A. Personal lust is always _____.
B. The biggest hang up is wanting it our _____.
C. We pray but ask for all of the _____ reasons.
D. Fighting occurs when we are out of _____.
E. Praying to God requires the right _____.

The Training Op

1. Can selfish motives hinder your prayers?
2. Why do you think that this is the case?
3. Read Joshua 24:15. Discuss it.

The Basics: Rom. 6:23-Discuss it. Memorize it.

Prepare For Battle: Closing Prayer

Daily Devotionals Week 4

-Day 1-

Fight To Be Faithful!

<u>*OPERATIONS MANUAL*</u>

Ye adulterers and adulteresses, know ye not that the friendship of the world is enmity with God? Whosoever therefore will be a friend of the world is the enemy of God. (James 4:4)

<u>*STRATEGIC INTELLIGENCE*</u>

Espionage is wicked. It suggests that there is a traitor in the camp. One who would appear to be with us but secretly be against us. The language here is very intimate and personal. In fact, James calls some believers adulterers and adulteresses. These people appear to love one person but have found it in their hearts to be intimate with someone else. It is cheating at its best.

James says the world is what God pulled you out of and you have been having a secret affair with the world and God cannot stand it any longer.

Here is the honest truth; no one wants to be cheated on. We desire faithfulness in our relationships and so does God. The Lord loves the faithful servant and the faithful believer and most importantly, a faithful soldier.

To be faithful does not suggest human perfection. However, what it does suggest is a spiritual connection that says I have chosen to live for Christ and I am not going to ever change my mind.

THE INWARD BATTLE

The word "world" used by James is cosmos. It means any system developed that leaves God out. List some systems in our day and time that try to leave God out of them?

In a more practical sense, the world also connotes and suggests places that you go that you do not want God to see you frequent. Do you have any worldly places that you frequent?

The world lures us and causes us to make God feel cheated on. After reading this devotional what are some things that you will plan to do differently?

TACTICAL WEAPONS AND WARFARE

Lord Jesus you have been faithful to me and I want to be faithful to you. Forgive me for anything that I have ever done that caused you grief as you watched me do it. I pray even now that my faithfulness towards you never be diminished but always heightened. Cause my love for you to overflow and my faithfulness to increase. In the name of Jesus, Amen!

-Day 2-

Fight With Grace!

OPERATIONS MANUAL

Do ye think that the scripture saith in vain, The spirit that dwelleth in us lusteth to envy? But he giveth more grace. Wherefore he saith, God resisteth the proud, but giveth grace unto the humble. (James 4:5-6)

STRATEGIC INTELLIGENCE

This is one of the greatest passages in the entire Bible. Let us begin this moment of meditation with this question in mind: why hasn't God given up on you yet? After all, you know right from wrong and still chose wrong from time to time. There are moments that you seek to stand for the Lord and end up falling by the wayside. In addition, to make matters worse, there are times when God literally feels betrayed by you. Why hasn't God just filed for a divorce and walked away from the relationship that He desires most from you?

Here is the answer that should melt your heart and make you want to fall at the Lord's feet and weep tears of joy. James says, "he giveth more grace."

Are you rejoicing yet? If not, you should be! The reason God has decided to keep you is not that you are flawless and perfect but that His grace has proven to be sufficient once again.

Thank God for grace!

THE INWARD BATTLE

Have you ever had a moment in your life when you did not feel like you were worthy to be called a Christian anymore?

Have you ever known better but chose poorly and made of mess of your life? What happened?

According to this devotional lesson, why has God not discarded you and sought to give His love to someone else?

TACTICAL WEAPONS AND WARFARE

O God of heaven thoughts of your grace brings me to tears. Thoughts of your love for me, bring me to my knees. Lord, I cannot say thank you enough for all that you mean to me. My cry today is to simply say thank you for the amazing, life changing grace that you have granted me! You have changed my life forever! In Jesus' name, I praise and petition you, Amen!

-Day 3-

Fight Against Enemy!

OPERATIONS MANUAL

Submit yourselves therefore to God. Resist the devil, and he will flee from you. (James 4:7)

STRATEGIC INTELLIGENCE

As believers in Christ Jesus, it is very important for you to understand that we have a very real enemy. He is the devil, Satan, Lucifer, the Anti-Christ, the evil one. He is dangerous and powerful. However, the shout of the lesson is that when compared to your God he is like a gnat in the face of a giant! Yes, the devil is our adversary, but Jesus Christ is our advocate and He has no equal in heaven, earth, or hell. He stands in a category all by Himself.

With this in mind, James gives two principles that will grant you victory when used in spiritual combat every single time.

It is very simple. Submit yourself to God and resist the devil! That is it. Do not let anyone complicate this for you. Submission means to surrender to God. To live life His way and not your way. It means to join His army, report for duty and follow His commands.

Secondly, we are told to resist the devil. The word resist is very interesting. It is the word we use to make the term antihistamine with. During cold and flu season people suffer from allergies. It is because in the air there is an overload of histamines. So in order for you to stand outside and not sneeze you have to take an antihistamine. It empowers you to stand while others are sneezing.

Get this; you do not defeat the enemy by using a prayer cloth. You defeat him by filling yourself with something that will allow you to stand while others are falling! Moreover, that something is the Word of God!

THE INWARD BATTLE

Take a real look at your life. Are you in complete submission to Jesus Christ? If not, why not start right now?

Has the enemy ever attacked you and you knew it was the devil behind it? What happened?

How does James say the enemy should be handled?

TACTICAL WEAPONS AND WARFARE

Lord my life has seen many attacks of the enemy and you have brought me through each of them. God I pray right now that you would empower me and endow me with more wisdom from your Word than ever before. God I desire to resist the enemy and His advances and I am declaring victory over my life according to what you have already promised me! In the name of Jesus, I ask it all, Amen!

-Day 4-

Fight To Be In His Presence!

OPERATIONS MANUAL

Draw nigh to God, and he will draw nigh to you. Cleanse your hands, ye sinners; and purify your hearts, ye double minded. (James 4:8)

STRATEGIC INTELLIGENCE

There is no greater blessing in the life of a soldier in the United States Military than to meet the Commander and Chief personally. To shake his hand and stand in his presence is an esteemed honor. Not long ago I had the pleasure to be in the company of a veteran that was blessed to meet President Clinton during his first term. He told me how excited he was to meet him and while sharing his story tears began falling down his cheek. He met the President.

Ponder this thought for a moment. What will it be like to meet God? I mean, to be in His presence. I am sure that no one will be standing. I am certain of this because Paul declares that *"...every knee shall bow....and every tongue shall confess that He is Lord to the glory of God the Father." (Phil. 2:10-11).*

James says there are some things that you will have to do before you can be considered. He says draw nigh to God, cleanse your hands, and make up your mind to live for Him. Draw nigh to God is actually temple talk. It could be rendered like this, go beyond the veil. It means desire to get into His presence. The notion of clean hands is a portrait of a priest washing in the laver. It suggests that sanctification is still the prerequisite for being in the presence of a Holy God and finally he says to get rid of your double mind. In short, make up your mind that you want Him and nothing else.

If meeting the President brings a man to tears, meeting God must be something that will change His life forever!

THE INWARD BATTLE

Imagine for a moment as you are sharing this devotional lesson that God is standing right above you smiling upon you as you study. Take a moment and whisper words of endearment to Him.

Be honest, could you be closer to God in your walk with Him? What are some of the things that may be stopping you?

Read St. Matthew 11:28. When you hear these Words spoken by Jesus what do they say to you?

TACTICAL WEAPONS AND WARFARE

God I love you. You mean everything to me. In your presence is healing. In your presence is love and power. In your presence is you! God I desire you more than I desire anything. I am drawing near to you because I want you near me. Thank you Lord for being a present help at all times. I bless you and I praise you for being my God. In Jesus' name, Amen!

-Day 5-

Fight Like A Soldier!

<u>OPERATIONS MANUAL</u>

Be afflicted, and mourn, and weep: let your laughter be turned to mourning, and your joy to heaviness. (James 4:9)

<u>STRATEGIC INTELLIGENCE</u>

When people enter the military they walk in as civilians but they are trained to become soldiers. From the first day of training, until they are discharged or retire they are taught to endure. They are trained to fight to the finish. Soldiers are those men and women who fight to the end. A soldier may be wounded on the field of battle, but they fight on; they may even have to mourn the loss of a fallen comrade, but they fight on; they often weep silent tears that no one can see, but they fight on. To persevere is the name of the game.

Likewise, for the believer in Jesus Christ who fights under the blood-stained banner of the cross, we too fight like a soldier. Weep if you must, but never stop fighting, endure your moments of hurt but get back up on your feet and fight on, and if death finds your family lament over your loss, thank God for what is left and fight to the finish!

Here is the Biblical principle that you should gain from this devotional segment of James, fight like a soldier! Persevere and endure until the end!

THE INWARD BATTLE

Have you ever had a moment when life got the best of you and you wanted to quit? What happened?

Take a moment to consider this devotional thought. You have endured until right now and you are still standing. You have been attacked, knocked down and in some cases left for dead, but you are still here. Why?

Read Psalms 121:1-3. What does it mean to you for God to be your help?

TACTICAL WEAPONS AND WARFARE

God there have been times in my life where I have grown weary. In those moments, I discovered just how wonderful you really are. When I was too weak to continue you carried me through and I know it. Thank you for being my strength when I had no strength left. Lord, my fighting is not over, so in days to come be my shield, my vicarious victor and my spiritual victory. In the name of the one who conquered the grave, in Jesus' name, Amen!

Group Encounter Week 5

FIGHT FOR YOUR RANK AND PROMOTION
James 4:10

Intelligence Briefing

1. Have prayer with your group.
2. Define humility and discuss what it is.
3. What has happened when you have used it?

Five Battle Strategies: Video Presentation

A. Humility means to become _____.
B. If you demote yourself God will _____ you.
C. The opposite of humility is _____.
D. Pride causes _____.
E. Humility is a _____ that you make.

The Training Op

1. Why does God love the humble?
2. Why does God resists the proud?
3. How does humility happen?

The Basics: 1 Pet. 5:6-7-Discuss it. Memorize it.

Prepare For Battle: Closing Prayer

Daily Devotionals Week 5

-Day 1-

Fight For Those Fighting With You!

OPERATIONS MANUAL

Speak not evil one of another, brethren. He that speaketh evil of his brother, and judgeth his brother, speaketh evil of the law, and judgeth the law: but if thou judge the law, thou art not a doer of the law, but a judge. (James 4:11)

STRATEGIC INTELLIGENCE

There is no way for you to fight against a common enemy if you are fighting against the people you are supposed to be fighting with. Internal strife is a kingdom killer. It destroys families, friendships and Christian fellowships like nothing else can. Often times it manifests itself when people that should be fighting for each other start speaking evil of each other instead of encouraging one another. The result is internal confusion regarding those that are around you and personal dislike for those that are nearest you. When this happens, everyone loses. They lose and you lose.

Do not fight against other believers, fight with them. Unity brings strength, harmony procures productivity, synergy promotes power, loyalty cements relationships, transparency does away with secrecy, and honesty mixed with integrity produces spiritual victory.

Keep this in mind, just because some believers are different does not mean that you have to reject them. Different is not bad, it is just different. If we fight together, there is no way that we can lose!

THE INWARD BATTLE

One of the greatest tricks of the enemy is to get believers to turn on each other. Have you ever seen this happen before? What took place?

Interestingly, the blessing of the Lord happens when believers that are different learn to love one another. Whom do you have in your life that is just hard to love? What is placing a strain on the relationship?

Judgmental believers are very dangerous. Have you ever been the subject of personal judgment before?

Be honest, have you ever inwardly or verbally been judgmental regarding someone? Why?

How has getting closer to Jesus Christ helped you with this matter?

TACTICAL WEAPONS AND WARFARE

Lord of heaven and God of glory, I know that division is of the enemy and I have decided never to let the enemy win again. I pray for the ability, fortitude, and magnitude to produce love and unity in all of my relationships, starting at home and reaching to everyone else. Bless you O God and I praise your name for what you are doing in my life regarding this matter. In the name of Jesus Christ, Amen!

-Day 2-

Fight, But Leave The Criticism Out Of It!

OPERATIONS MANUAL

There is one lawgiver, who is able to save and to destroy: who art thou that judgest another? (James 4:12)

STRATEGIC INTELLIGENCE

Have you ever noticed that people that are very critical of others are never ever critical of themselves? Imagine what life would look like if we were never able to be critical of others until we first got ourselves together. Wouldn't that be wonderful? Unfortunately, that is not how it works. Often times we are very demeaning and critical of everyone.

Keep this in mind, even if a criticism is true, if given in the wrong spirit can cause more harm than good. James argues his point by saying "who are you to start judging others?" In short, strong soldiers keep their criticisms to themselves and share their exhortations of others with everyone.

THE INWARD BATTLE

It is easy to judge others because you place all of your attention on them and not on you. Be honest what are some things you need to correct today?

Do you have the courage and strength to correct these things?

The Greatest Commandment is to love others and not to be critical of them. Read St. John 13:34. What do these words say to your heart?

TACTICAL WEAPONS AND WARFARE

Lord there has been times when I have been extremely critical of others. There have even been times when I have made my criticisms known and to be honest, I have hurt some people with my words. God I am not perfect, but I earnestly ask that you forgive me and help me to speak well of people and to encourage them along the way. Do it in me for your glory. In the name of my risen Savior Jesus Christ, I petition you, Amen!

-Day 3-

Fight Like All That You Have Is Today!

<u>*OPERATIONS MANUAL*</u>

Go to now, ye that say, To day or to morrow we will go into such a city, and continue there a year, and buy and sell, and get gain: whereas ye know not what shall be on the morrow. For what is your life? It is even a vapour, that appeareth for a little time, and then vanisheth away. (James 4:13-14)

<u>*STRATEGIC INTELLIGENCE*</u>

Today is the first day of the rest of your life. You have never seen it before and you will never ever see it again. If you waste it, you will lose it. If you mistreat it and abuse it, you will miss the wonderful opportunity to use it. Get busy. Get started! Today is here right now. A real soldier understands that tomorrow is not promised. All you have is today! That is it. Not next week, not next month, not next year, you have the gift of today. Use it wisely.

Yesterday and all of its splendor and failures are behind you. They are buried in the leftover sea of the past. With this in mind, do not let your past failures determine your future productivity. Yesterday is now your history. Do not relish over your great successes that were accomplished yesterday either. Yesterday's win does not amount to victory on today. Each day stands on its own.

Today is a new day! Live it in Christ Jesus to the fullest!

THE INWARD BATTLE

There are times your past failures can haunt you. Has this ever happened to you?

There are times that your past victories can stunt future wins. Have you ever been there?

What can you do for the Lord starting today that you have never done before?

Here is the best advice ever, do it!

TACTICAL WEAPONS AND WARFARE

God there have been moments, times and seasons when I have just wasted days doing absolutely nothing. Please forgive me. Lord from now on I plan to live the life that you give me to the fullest. I plan to pray more, read the Bible more, and serve you more than I have before in my life. Empower me with your spirit, exhort me through your Word, and embrace me with your strength is my earnest plea. In Jesus' name, Amen!

-Day 4-

Fight Against Taking Life For Granted!

OPERATIONS MANUAL

For that ye ought to say, If the Lord will, we shall live, and do this, or that. But now ye rejoice in your boastings: all such rejoicing is evil. (James 4:15-16)

STRATEGIC INTELLIGENCE

You are alive today. That is obvious because you are reading this devotional on the book of James. However, here is the question that is worth billions, will you be alive tomorrow? Here is the honest answer and the hard to swallow truth, you have no idea! All too often, we look at tomorrow as if it is a guarantee. Hear this wisdom sent from heaven, it is not.

James describes human life as a brief puff of smoke rising from the altar. It is visible only for a moment and then it disappears. All of us who travel through time towards eternity are just like brief clouds of smoke, here today and gone tomorrow. James gives us these words to caution us to never take tomorrow as a guarantee and to command us to live each day to its fullest in the Lord.

Make plans for tomorrow, but make them knowing that there is a strong possibility that you just might not be there to see any of them. Moreover, if God is gracious enough to let you see tomorrow, get there with a smile on your face, gratitude in your heart and a thank you in your spirit.

THE INWARD BATTLE

Have you heard the old folks say "if the Lord will?" What does this statement mean to you?

Has God ever let you make your plans for your the future and then change all of them? What happened?

Read St. Luke 12:16-21. How does this parable make you feel?

TACTICAL WEAPONS AND WARFARE

God I am alive and I am grateful! I have been through many situations that should have taken me out, but I am still standing and for that I give you glory. I will not take tomorrow for granted but I will live in your amazing grace of today all day long. I am so thankful. In Jesus' name, Amen!

-Day 5-

Fight To Do The Right Thing!

OPERATIONS MANUAL

Therefore to him that knoweth to do good, and doeth it not, to him it is sin. (James 4:17)

STRATEGIC INTELLIGENCE

To know what is right and do what is right is wise. To know what is right and do what is wrong is ignorant. Okay, let us be honest for a moment. We have all been on the ignorant list a time or two. On the other hand, maybe even more times than we care to mention. However, there comes a time when God is expecting you to know better and do better because of what you know.

James is speaking in an emphatic voice here. He is screaming this one phrase for everyone to hear him, do the right thing! If forgiveness is right, do it! If tithing is right, do it! If the worship of our Lord is right, do it! If serving the Lord is right, then do it! If praying for those that need healing is right, do it! And if obeying the Lord God Almighty is right, do it!

Fight to do what is right and what is right will fix your fight and lead you to victory in the end!

THE INWARD BATTLE

To do what is wrong is sin. Please know that sin is very dangerous and should never be taken lightly. What are some sins that you need to get rid of today? What are you waiting for?

Read Romans 6:23. What is the difference between "wages" and a "gift"? Here is some wisdom for you, take the gift.

TACTICAL WEAPONS AND WARFARE

Lord there are times that I know better, but I do not do any better. I lean on grace and rely on mercy. Though grace and mercy are more than enough, I want to do better so that my decisions are never to knowingly make a mistake. I hate sin and I love you. God help me in every area of my life to fight to do the right thing. Thank you for your love that never fails and your kindness that never ceases. In the name of He who died for my sins, Jesus Christ, Amen!

Group Encounter Week 6

FIGHT KNOWING IT IS HIS AND NOT YOURS
James 5:1-4

Intelligence Briefing

1. Welcome your group and whisper a prayer.
2. Discuss what it means to be a steward.
3. Is there a difference between rich and wealthy? Discuss this for a moment.

Five Battle Strategies: Video Presentation

A. The _____ feel they earned it without God.
B. The wealthy are _____ and know it.
C. When you die your _____ will stay here.
D. Rich people think that money is _____.
E. The cry of the _____ will always reach God.

The Training Op

1. Do you know what it is like to be poor?
2. Has God ever not taken care of you?
3. Is it possible to be rich with no money?

The Basics: Psalms 23-Discuss it. Memorize it.

Prepare For Battle: Closing Prayer

Daily Devotionals Week 6

-Day 1-

Fight Off Human pride!

<u>*OPERATIONS MANUAL*</u>

Ye have lived in pleasure on the earth, and been wanton; ye have nourished your hearts, as in a day of slaughter. Ye have condemned and killed the just; and he doth not resist you. (James 5:5-6)

<u>*STRATEGIC INTELLIGENCE*</u>

Human pride is dangerous. It will make you think that you are more than what you really are. Pride does not just show up and take over. It is sneaky, subtle, and smooth. Pride flies in under the radar of your life and in many ways is completely unnoticeable. In fact, people that have pride problems rarely know that their pride is a problem.

James warns the Jewish converts that are scattered abroad about living well while others suffer and yet paying no attention to those who are less fortunate. He cautions those who look like they have it all but still have nothing. Isn't it amazing, people who often have money and resources but lack God need more stuff to make them happy. In addition, people with little money and a whole lot of God are happy with Him and do not need much stuff.

Here is the bottom line, pride leaves you longing for things on earth and humility places you in the lap of the Lord who is in heaven, who meets your every need.

Help those who cannot help themselves, be thankful for what you have and when your increase comes do not forget who gave you everything that you possess!

THE INWARD BATTLE

Here is how you can sense pride and detect it early:

1. Do you think that you are just a little better than other people are?
2. Do you look down on people that have less than you do?
3. Do you occasionally forget where God brought you from?

If you answered yes to any of these questions you might have a pride problem.

TACTICAL WEAPONS AND WARFARE

Lord I cannot ever forget what you have done for me and from whence you have brought me from. I do not have room for human pride because I know that without you I am absolutely nothing. Lord help me to bless those who have less than I do and expect nothing in return. God I know that pride is sneaky so please I pray; help me to fight it off! I pray this petition in the name of Jesus Christ, Amen!

-Day 2-

Fight With Patience!

OPERATIONS MANUAL

Be patient therefore, brethren, unto the coming of the Lord. Behold, the husbandman waiteth for the precious fruit of the earth, and hath long patience for it, until he receive the early and latter rain. Be ye also patient; stablish your hearts: for the coming of the Lord draweth nigh. (James 5:7-8)

STRATEGIC INTELLIGENCE

People in the military are persons who are long suffering. They are tough. You cannot be made from tissue paper and think that you will make a good soldier. Real soldiers are hardcore. The greatest men and women of the United States Military forces are those who have fought on when fighting no longer made any sense. They are brave, courageous, and faithful. This is the exhortation that James gives in these verses. He encourages the believers to be long-suffering and endure until the Lord returns.

In short, a true believer in the Lord Jesus Christ has to fight until they cannot fight anymore. And, even then, we are told to fight on!

Endure! Persevere! Do not faint! Do not quit! Fight to the end!

THE INWARD BATTLE

The Lord is going to return one day in His Second Coming. Read St. Matt. 24:4-14.

Often times patience is not our greatest asset. How has patience ever blessed you?

Endurance and patience suggest never giving up. What are some things that you are enduring right now?

TACTICAL WEAPONS AND WARFARE

Lord give me more patience and help me endure until the very end. Give me your strength when I get weak and give me a refill of your spirit when I am running low. I am here to serve you and you alone. Keep me strong in battle and patient regarding your coming. In Jesus' name, Amen!

-Day 3-

Fight Through The Pain!

OPERATIONS MANUAL

Grudge not one against another, brethren, lest ye be condemned: behold, the judge standeth before the door. Take, my brethren, the prophets, who have spoken in the name of the Lord, for an example of suffering affliction, and of patience. Behold, we count them happy which endure. Ye have heard of the patience of Job, and have seen the end of the Lord; that the Lord is very pitiful, and of tender mercy. But above all things, my brethren, swear not, neither by heaven, neither by the earth, neither by any other oath: but let your yea be yea; and your nay, nay; lest ye fall into condemnation. (James 5:9-12)

STRATEGIC INTELLIGENCE

Suffering and affliction are intricate parts of the journey of life for everyone. You will not make it through this life without weeping some tears from time to time. For the child of God who loves the Lord dearly it will happen, I promise you that.

James is so confident that it will happen that he reminds us of Job. The godly man from the Land of Uz, who was tested beyond human imagination with the death of all ten of his kids, the loss of his earthly wealth and health that went from good to inhumane in just a few days. Here is the point, if Job suffered and was afflicted it will also happen to you. No one is exempt, no one.

Therefore, there comes a time in your life when you must fight through the pain. You have to keep pressing your way even when your way seems dreary and things seem unfair.

Say what you mean, mean what you say, stand for the Lord and He will always stand for you.

THE INWARD BATTLE

Have you ever had to suffer? Reflect on that time in your life?
What did you learn about God?
How did you endure the whole ordeal?

TACTICAL WEAPONS AND WARFARE

O God I have been hurt so many times and had to suffer through many things. Each time I was afflicted I learned more and more about you. Today I am alive because you are not through blessing me. Use my life to bring you ultimate glory and make me strong for the race that is still yet ahead. In Jesus' name, Amen!

-Day 4-

Fight Like A Warrior In Prayer!

OPERATIONS MANUAL

Is any among you afflicted? let him pray. Is any merry? let him sing psalms. Is any sick among you? let him call for the elders of the church; and let them pray over him, anointing him with oil in the name of the Lord: and the prayer of faith shall save the sick, and the Lord shall raise him up; and if he have committed sins, they shall be forgiven him. Confess your faults one to another, and pray one for another, that ye may be healed. The effectual fervent prayer of a righteous man availeth much. Elias was a man subject to like passions as we are, and he prayed earnestly that it might not rain: and it rained not on the earth by the space of three years and six months. And he prayed again, and the heaven gave rain, and the earth brought forth her fruit. (James 5:13-18)

STRATEGIC INTELLIGENCE

Prayer still works! When you are in enemy territory, you must pray. When the sun is shining on your life, you need to pray. When all seems to be failing around you, please stop and pray. When you are at a point where you must make a life changing decision, please pause to pray. Prayer! It is the secret weapon of every believer on the battlefield of our God!

James informs the people of God that there is a way to heal the sick and it is with the prayers of the righteous that avail much. The idea behind prayers that avail is the reality that in prayer we must prevail. Never ever stop praying. There is even a time when we should call for the Elders of the church and ask them to pray. This is not done because their prayers have more power than your prayers do. This is done so that the Elders can bear witness to the fact that God's power is supreme and like none other.

Here is the key to spiritual victory that unbelieving hearts will never ever understand, prayer really does work!

THE INWARD BATTLE

Read 1 Thess. 5:17. What does this say to you?

Read 2 Chronicles 7:14. Can you hear God in this verse? What does it say to your heart?

Read St. Matthew 6:9-13. Commit this prayer to memory if you have not done so already.

TACTICAL WEAPONS AND WARFARE

God I know that prayer still works but I want to increase my prayer life and pray like a strong warrior who fights spiritual battles and wins them. God thank you for the confirmations of your Word that you really do answer prayer and I thank you for the prayers that you have answered for me in my life. I am honored that you hear me and I am overwhelmed to know that you answer me. I bless you in prayer even now, in Jesus' name, Amen!

-Day 5-

Fight Never To Leave Soldier Behind!

<u>*OPERATIONS MANUAL*</u>

Brethren, if any of you do err from the truth, and one convert him; let him know, that he which converteth the sinner from the error of his way shall save a soul from death, and shall hide a multitude of sins. (James 5:18-19)

<u>*STRATEGIC INTELLIGENCE*</u>

Never ever, leave a soldier behind. That is the rule! You live and die by this rule. If a soldier is fallen, you return and get him. Carry him on your shoulders, lift him in your arms, do whatever you have to do to get him to safety, but never leave another soldier behind!

We have it bad. We leave people behind all of the time. We leave brothers, sisters, in-laws, friends, coworkers, neighbors, classmates, schoolmates, fraternity brothers, sorority sisters, and even enemies behind when it comes to salvation. However, redemption must be radical! It is like snatching someone out of the jaws of death and saving their lives.

James concludes his letter by declaring do not leave anyone on the battlefield! In short, there is still room at the cross for sinners like you and me! If God did it for us, He could do it and even more for them!

Remember this, Jesus still saves, and He wants you to rescue those that you know need Him and bring them to His bleeding side. There they will find a life that lasts forever!

THE INWARD BATTLE

Make a list of all of the people that you love. Make sure the list is complete.

How many of the people on your list are unsaved?

Pray for the salvation of those that are unsaved as if your life depends on it. Ask God to save them.

If possible, contact them and share your faith in Christ with them.

TACTICAL WEAPONS AND WARFARE

Lord my prayer as I conclude this six weeks study of the book of James is that you would save everybody that I have ever seen with my eyes on earth. No matter where I saw them, my prayer is that you would save them. Let the same grace that saved me reach them. Do for them what you have done for me. In the name of Jesus who is Lord and Christ, I make this plea, Amen!

BATTLE STRATEGIES
ANSWER KEY

Group Session 1
1. JOY
2. GOD
3. TOUGH
4. PERFECT
5. GOD

Group Session 2
1. WORD
2. HEAR
3. MAN
4. ALWAYS
5. FAITH

Group Session 3
1. TEACHERS
2. WORDS
3. PORELY
4. MOUTH
5. SAY

Group Session 4
1. DANGEROUS
2. WAY
3. WRONG
4. OPTIONS
5. SPIRIT

Group Session 5
1. LOW
2. PROMOTE
3. PRIDE
4. DESTRUCTION
5. DECISION

Group Session 6
1. RICH
2. BLESSED
3. MONEY
4. EVERYTHING
5. POOR

About the Author

Dr. John R. Adolph

Dr. John R. Adolph is a called servant of God and one of the greatest voices in the body of Christ for this generation. He is the Senior Pastor of Antioch Missionary Baptist Church in Beaumont, Texas. He often serves as an evangelist for revivals and crusades; he is an author, a sought-after conference speaker, and well-established community leader.

Dr. Adolph is a proud graduate of M. B. Smiley Senior High School in Houston, Texas earning his diploma; Texas Southern University earning his B.B.A. with a concentration in Finance and Accounting, the Interdenominational Theological Center, Morehouse School of Religion earning his MDIV with a concentration in Pastoral Care and Counseling, Houston Graduate School of Theology with a Doctor of Ministry Degree and the Oxford Round Table, Oxford, England.

Dr. Adolph serves as the President of Exalting the Savior Ministries, LLC, a nationally recognized organization that seeks to empower the people of God spiritually, economically, socially, relationally, and physically. He currently streams to a waiting web-based congregation of thousands and preaches to millions via IMPAC Broadcasting Network and TBN Broadcasting Network in Jefferson County, Texas.

Dr. Adolph has authored several books to include *Victorious Christian Living, Vol. 1 & 2, Let Me Encourage You, I'm Coming*

Out of This; Marriage is for Losers and Celibacy is for Fools and I'm Changing the Game.

Dr. Adolph serves on the Board of Trustees of Baptist Hospital, the I Have A Dream Program of Beaumont, Texas, the President of Jehovah Jireh Village, and the Board of Directors for the National Baptist Convention, USA, Inc.

He has faithfully served at Antioch for 19 years and has seen the Lord grow the congregation from 250 to a faith-fellowship of well over 9,000. The current ministry campus consists of over 120,000 square feet of plant and facility, a beautiful neighborhood called Jehovah Jireh Village I & II, a townhouse development called Grace Lakes which is now home to over 140 residents and Dr. Adolph is currently working to implement an academic institution for children called the Royal Ambassador Academy.

Dr. Adolph is married to the love of his life Dorrie Eileen and is the proud father of two great kids, Sumone Elizabeth and Jonathan Raeshawn.